SCRIPTURE SCRIBBLES III

SCRIPTURE SCRIBBLES III: CARTOONS FROM THE CHOIR LOFT

PHILLIP DILLMAN

Copyright © 2016 by Phillip Dillman

All rights reserved. No part of this book may be used or reproduced in any manner whatsoever without written permission, except in the case of brief quotations embodied in critical articles or reviews.

Published 2016 by HumorOutcasts Press
Printed in the United States of America

ISBN-10: 0-9980899-3-1
ISBN-13: 978-0-9980899-3-5

ACKNOWLEDGMENTS

I need to say a special thank you (a bit late) to my cousin, Terry Dillman Lennox Wiza, who suggested that I contact Donna Cavanagh at HumorOutcasts Publishing and also to Donna for adding me to her group of talented authors and in her belief that her readers would enjoy my scribbles as much as she does. Also, thank you Jesus for still being a good sport about my varied portrayals of him.

More Scripture Scribbles: Cartoons from the Choir Loft

Introduction

It's hard to believe that this is my third book of Scripture Scribbles, already! I used to worry about running out of ideas for these cartoons, probably in the same way that a preacher hopes to find a fresh approach for a familiar scripture that they are preaching on for the fifteenth time! Fortunately, God continues to surprise me and inspire me with ideas which allow me to draw with a sense of purpose. Whether that purpose is to help the reader look at a familiar Bible passage with fresh eyes or to simply make them laugh, I know that I'm not drawing for me. Rather, my scribbles are for the sake of others.

I consider myself to be a "late bloomer." Common sense, street smarts, wisdom, or whatever you want to call it, developed much later for me than for my peers. Yet, academically, I wasn't too far behind. It just took me an additional couple of decades to be able to work with words well enough to be humorous on paper or to be able to conjure images with words. Sometimes, I can even get the words and images to cooperate in a drawing!

My experiences while growing up probably ran parallel to most people's lives throughout the 1960s through the 1980s. In the area of entertainment, I watched Saturday morning cartoons like Bugs Bunny and Roadrunner (Looney Tunes cartoons are my favorite!), Scooby Doo, Fat Albert, etc. I also spent time reading comic books like Peanuts (Charlie Brown, etc), Dennis the Menace, and the Archie comics. The only part of the newspaper that interested me were the comics pages, especially Bloom County and The Far Side. I eventually discovered the macabre and twisted humor of Chas Addams cartoons which inspired the creation of the television series called "The Addams Family." Another segment of my twisted sense of humor came from watching "Monty Python's Flying Circus" on the Public Television station in Chicago. My guess is that all of those influences are swirling around deep in the recesses of my mind and that anything new that enters my head is forced to wander through that unsettling portion of my brain until it is finally allowed to filter out through my pen and onto a folded-over piece of paper. Admittedly, some of the inspirations are arrested before reaching the paper due to possibly being deemed "inappropriate" for younger or more sensitive viewers. HA!

As I have become more confident in my ability to convey a message through my scribbles, and since I need more than 100 scribbles for each book, I now make sure that I have plenty of blank paper with me in the truck that I drive so that I can draw some of my cartoons while my trailer is being loaded or unloaded. It actually makes the truck-driving job a bit more tolerable! Many of the scribbles are still drawn during church, though. As I share that day's drawings during the "Heavenly Perks" coffee hour following the church service, I am often introduced to visitors as the church's "resident cartoonist." I really don't consider myself a cartoonist as much as I see myself as a truck driver that scribbles scriptural images to make people laugh, think, or both!

More Scripture Scribbles: Cartoons from the Choir Loft

Old Testament: The Beginning

More Scripture Scribbles: Cartoons from the Choir Loft

More Scripture Scribbles: Cartoons from the Choir Loft

More Scripture Scribbles: Cartoons from the Choir Loft

Phillip Dillman

More Scripture Scribbles: Cartoons from the Choir Loft

More Scripture Scribbles: Cartoons from the Choir Loft

More Scripture Scribbles: Cartoons from the Choir Loft

Phillip Dillman

More Scripture Scribbles: Cartoons from the Choir Loft

New Testament

More Scripture Scribbles: Cartoons from the Choir Loft

More Scripture Scribbles: Cartoons from the Choir Loft

Phillip Dillman

More Scripture Scribbles: Cartoons from the Choir Loft

More Scripture Scribbles: Cartoons from the Choir Loft

More Scripture Scribbles: Cartoons from the Choir Loft

More Scripture Scribbles: Cartoons from the Choir Loft

More Scripture Scribbles: Cartoons from the Choir Loft

More Scripture Scribbles: Cartoons from the Choir Loft

More Scripture Scribbles: Cartoons from the Choir Loft

More Scripture Scribbles: Cartoons from the Choir Loft

More Scripture Scribbles: Cartoons from the Choir Loft

More Scripture Scribbles: Cartoons from the Choir Loft

More Scripture Scribbles: Cartoons from the Choir Loft

More Scripture Scribbles: Cartoons from the Choir Loft

More Scripture Scribbles: Cartoons from the Choir Loft

More Scripture Scribbles: Cartoons from the Choir Loft

More Scripture Scribbles: Cartoons from the Choir Loft

More Scripture Scribbles: Cartoons from the Choir Loft

More Scripture Scribbles: Cartoons from the Choir Loft

More Scripture Scribbles: Cartoons from the Choir Loft

More Scripture Scribbles: Cartoons from the Choir Loft

Holy Holidays

More Scripture Scribbles: Cartoons from the Choir Loft

More Scripture Scribbles: Cartoons from the Choir Loft

HE HEARD THE HYMN "WHEN THE SAINTS GO MARCHING IN." NOW, HE THINKS THAT "SAINT NICK" HAS TO JOIN THE ARMY AND MISS CHRISTMAS!
WHAAAA
HYMNS
11.24.15

More Scripture Scribbles: Cartoons from the Choir Loft

More Scripture Scribbles: Cartoons from the Choir Loft

More Scripture Scribbles: Cartoons from the Choir Loft

More Scripture Scribbles: Cartoons from the Choir Loft

More Scripture Scribbles: Cartoons from the Choir Loft

Church Laughter

More Scripture Scribbles: Cartoons from the Choir Loft

More Scripture Scribbles: Cartoons from the Choir Loft

WHY, YES, SUZIE. I GUESS BEING BORN AGAIN AND HAVING ETERNAL LIFE IS GOD'S OWN RECYCLING PROGRAM!
RECYCLE
11.24.15

More Scripture Scribbles: Cartoons from the Choir Loft

More Scripture Scribbles: Cartoons from the Choir Loft

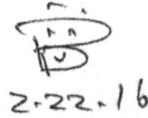

More Scripture Scribbles: Cartoons from the Choir Loft

More Scripture Scribbles: Cartoons from the Choir Loft

More Scripture Scribbles: Cartoons from the Choir Loft

More Scripture Scribbles: Cartoons from the Choir Loft

More Scripture Scribbles: Cartoons from the Choir Loft

More Scripture Scribbles: Cartoons from the Choir Loft

"I baptize you in the name of the Father, the Son, and the Holy Spirit, in water that has been tested and certified to be free of lead, harmful bacteria, and other contaminants, is P.H. balanced, and was used to make my morning cup of tea. Amen!"

More Scripture Scribbles: Cartoons from the Choir Loft

More Scripture Scribbles: Cartoons from the Choir Loft

More Scripture Scribbles: Cartoons from the Choir Loft

More Scripture Scribbles: Cartoons from the Choir Loft

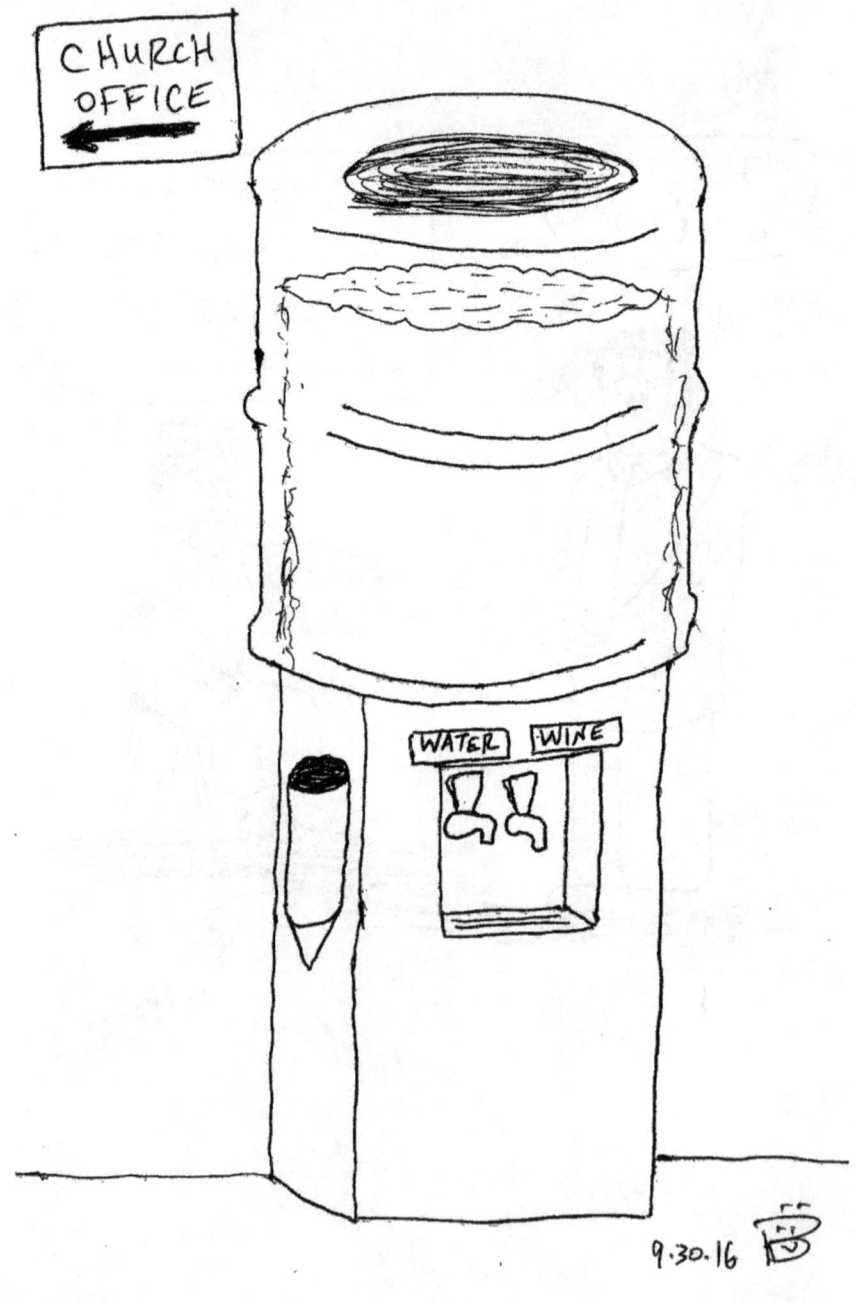

Everyday Life

More Scripture Scribbles: Cartoons from the Choir Loft

More Scripture Scribbles: Cartoons from the Choir Loft

More Scripture Scribbles: Cartoons from the Choir Loft

More Scripture Scribbles: Cartoons from the Choir Loft

More Scripture Scribbles: Cartoons from the Choir Loft

More Scripture Scribbles: Cartoons from the Choir Loft

More Scripture Scribbles: Cartoons from the Choir Loft

More Scripture Scribbles: Cartoons from the Choir Loft

More Scripture Scribbles: Cartoons from the Choir Loft

More Scripture Scribbles: Cartoons from the Choir Loft

More Scripture Scribbles: Cartoons from the Choir Loft

More Scripture Scribbles: Cartoons from the Choir Loft

More Scripture Scribbles: Cartoons from the Choir Loft

More Scripture Scribbles: Cartoons from the Choir Loft

God Almighty

More Scripture Scribbles: Cartoons from the Choir Loft

More Scripture Scribbles: Cartoons from the Choir Loft

More Scripture Scribbles: Cartoons from the Choir Loft

More Scripture Scribbles: Cartoons from the Choir Loft

Heaven

I'M HAVING TROUBLE SLEEPING HERE IN HEAVEN. MAYBE I SHOULD REQUEST A FIRMER CLOUD.
10.20.16

More Scripture Scribbles: Cartoons from the Choir Loft

More Scripture Scribbles: Cartoons from the Choir Loft

Characters in the Bible

More Scripture Scribbles: Cartoons from the Choir Loft

More Scripture Scribbles: Cartoons from the Choir Loft

The End

About the Author:

Phil Dillman was born and raised in Homewood, Illinois. His parents went to church regularly at First Presbyterian Church of Homewood, with Phil and his sister, Laura, regularly attending Sunday School. Phil remembers some of the drawings he did during that time, one being an erupting volcano. This was inspired by the topic of creation. He was thrilled when the drawings done by the kids in the class were projected onto the wall of the sanctuary during a church service later in the year. There, as big as life, was his image of a volcano spewing and streaming molten lava down its sides. That was cool!

Nearly forty years later, Phil sings in the choir and finds inspiration for his drawings in the scripture lessons or the sermons. Many of the drawings are humorous (at least to Phil) while some are a bit more serious. Some of the references are obvious while some are a bit abstract or absurd. Either way, it is hoped that everyone will enjoy the book and not be offended by any of it.

By the way, Phil really is listening to what is being said during the service!

Phil is a truck driver during the week and is the Editor of two quarterly newsletters; one for the Pepsi-Cola Collectors Club and one for the Dillman Family Association (genealogy). He co-authored a book on Pepsi Memorabilia in 2000. This book "More Scripture Scribbles", is the follow up to Phil's first book "Scripture Scribbles".

All of the artwork was done by Phil Dillman. The photo of Phil was taken by Craig Miller.

www.ingramcontent.com/pod-product-compliance
Lightning Source LLC
LaVergne TN
LVHW041617070426
835507LV00008B/301